The OCD Poems

The OCD Poems

Dennis Rhodes

INDOLENT BOOKS

Book design: adam b. bohannon

Book editor: Michael Broder

Published by Indolent Books,

an imprint of Indolent Arts Foundation, Inc.

www.indolentbooks.com

Brooklyn, New York

ISBN: 978-1-945023-27-9

Special thanks to Epic Sponsor Megan Chinburg for helping to fund
the production of this book.

For Scott,
my therapist,
my confidant,
my friend

CONTENTS

Foreword   XI

My Six Word Autobiography   3
Cousin Gloria   4
Retrospect   6
Untitled 12   7
Untitled 3   8
This Is Not a Pleasant Poem   9
OCD 3   10
This Is Not a Suicide Note   11
Roberto   12
One Week in My Life   13
OCD Blues   14
Plea of an Obsessive Compulsive Man   15
OCD, Explained   16
The Weight of Spring   17
Notwithstanding   18
Would-Be   19
Man Up   20
Untitled 7   21
Enough Said   22
Note to Therapist 1   23
Credo   24
April, 2010   25
Untitled 14   26
Bacon   27
At the Zoo   28
Dead of Night   29
Healing   30
Fear   31
Man With OCD on Ocean Liner   32

My Germs   33

My Psychotherapist   34

Note to Therapist 2   35

Obsessive Compulsive   36

Note to Therapist 3   38

Ode to Abilify   39

Reflection   40

This is OCD   41

OCD 2   42

Untitled 1   43

Untitled 13   44

A Dubious but Welcome Anniversary   45

End of an Era   46

Breakthrough   47

OCD (not)   48

No Clouds Today   49

OCD, Tamed   50

Factoid From the OCD Conference   51

Journal Notes: Anxiety   52

Untitled 4   53

Untitled 8   54

Untitled 11   55

Fires   56

OCD 1   57

Untitled 9   58

The Last OCD poem   59

Acknowledgments   61

Make the private world public, that's what the poet does.

ALLEN GINSBERG

FOREWORD

OCD is not funny.
OCD can be fatal.
OCD is Satan's favorite sport.
OCD is a cruel self-punishment.
OCD drains your spirit.
OCD stifles your soul.
OCD makes decent thoughts indecent.
OCD is an existential threat.
OCD is a fucking monster.
OCD is anything but poetic.
OCD sucks.

The OCD Poems

My Six Word Autobiography

Orphaned. Molested. OCD. HIV. Still here.

Cousin Gloria

My mother's cousin Gloria roamed the streets
of West New York, New Jersey for
thirty years in a cloud of mental illness;
talked to herself and no one else.
Her face, a riot of make-up like
a circus clown, she was known to all
as crazy, touched in the head.

Her mother, Alice, my mom's aunt
was not happy with a daughter
who was a public spectacle in the neighborhood.
Alice did not lack compassion, she
was just bewildered: this was the fifties.
It was shameful to be mentally ill.

Gloria had been married and divorced
And had a teen-age son who killed himself.
With little hope that Gloria would
emerge from her illness,
Alice, without the heart to send her away,
Let her wander the streets like a zombie.

My mother suffered two breakdowns
which sent her children to the orphanage.
That is how and why my OCD
took hold: I tried to have a sympathy
nervous breakdown without success.
I grew up largely on the right side
of sanity holding myself together
until middle age, when at 56 I
took a knife to my own throat,

whistled past the graveyard and
recovered with enough material
for three books of poetry.

I used to hate Anne Sexton and Sylvia Plath
for killing themselves.
It came as a rude shock that poets must do what
they must for the sake of their art.
These days I stay away from knives
and let my pen do my dirty work.

Retrospect

The first thing I did wrong
was to slip out of the womb
into this madness. Certainly
I had no choice but I can choose
to call it a mistake. This is
the thing: I seemed perfectly
normal. How could they not know
it was mental illness that
lurked in my genes and threatened
my quality of life, rode
my back day and night, wrestled
me to the ground. How could they
ignore the fact that half my
family were nut cases—how?

Untitled 12

The past is a bully.
It has no mercy.
It is a power unto itself.
It can pull you down like gravity.

The future—a question mark.
Nothing you need to know.
There is no guarantee
you will even have one.

The present—an enigma.
Our hearts beat relentlessly
for no apparent reason.
Knowing something we don't.

Untitled 3

I feel dead inside. Sometimes. For very brief periods. At
these times I perform a kind of emotional CPR on myself,
like jump-starting a stalled heart. I know why this happens:
the day I went to the orphanage it was like being killed.
In cold blood. And it was a sunny day, not the dark of night.
I had to jolt myself alive. I was going to hell and I could do
nothing about it. Quite a day. I knew then that my life would
always be a fight for mere survival. I knew then that happiness
would always be elusive. Poetry became my saving grace . . .
God gave me a tremendous affliction (OCD) but he also gave
me a modest genius: the wherewithal to fight my way out.

This Is Not a Pleasant Poem

There was a boy who washed his hands
and didn't know he'd washed his
hands. He did not think he had
washed his hands and so he washed
his hands again: he still
did not feel that he'd washed those
hands and no one could tell him
they were safely washed and so
he went on washing his hands til
his hands were red and raw but
never clean. There was a man
who took a knife and slit his throat
and flirted on the edge of death
but he could not die, he did not die
not while he had to wash his hands--
a little boy's work is never done.
There was a boy who washed his hands.

OCD 3

This is OCD, and my life:
Someone holding a gun
hands you a cup, says
"It's going to rain.
If any raindrops hit the ground,
you die."

In some perverse way,
you want to please him
so you take the cup
from the devil's hand
and await the rain—
risking the fatal
for the fleeting satisfaction
of the futile.

This Is Not a Suicide Note

You don't understand.
I am up here on this ledge
not because I want to kill
myself, but because I don't.
Please don't pray that I don't jump –
pray that I do, that I have
the balls to be Icarus
in reverse: to leap away
from the sun, with no false wings
and celebrate the limits
of my dumb humanity.

Just get out of my way.
Let me fall and fall and fall
blissfully, and forever.

Roberto

Roberto winces at his own thoughts.
They have complete control of him.
Something's gone wrong with his brain.
I know what he's going through. When I
was sixteen my brain went haywire:
I counted madly and banged my head
against a black cinder-block wall.
I had a need to align my whole being
with the straight, solid line I embraced
on that wall. Roberto is different.
My obsessions were suffered in secret.
His torment, unlike mine, is obvious.
I was stoic in my suffering.
I still am. Roberto's fingers cripple
as he struggles to express himself. He
flashes keen intelligence in his eyes.
Intelligence pulled me into OCD
and is slowly pulling me out of it.
Roberto's intelligence will save him
in the end. He will heal with a bitter grace.
I look away when I see him, unsure
if my tears are for myself or for him.
All I can do is set a good example.
Fight like hell, Roberto. Just like I did.

One Week in My Life

They gave us ice cream in the psych ward.
As much as we wanted. Perhaps
it was spiked with Valium or drugs
to raise our serotonin levels—
any time day or night we could go
to the fridge: chocolate the overwhelming
flavor of choice. One of us
was schizophrenic, another was
bipolar. I was the one ravaged
by OCD. One woman had eight
personalities. We were amused
that she took a cup for each of them.
I liked three of them. Disliked four others.
One of them was a complete lunatic.

OCD Blues

I have a soft spot for germs.
Can't tell you how many times
I've consoled one at some bar
or other. Their sob stories
get to me and touch my heart.
Used to fear them terribly.
They nearly ruined my childhood.
After years of therapy
I realized they mean no harm.
Sure, I could blame my mother
(doesn't everyone do that).
I could blame my pedophile
for making me neurotic.
But I kind of like germs. Now.

Plea of an Obsessive Compulsive Man

Please Please PLEASE no more things!
I weep with despair when someone brings
a well-intentioned book, some harmless toy –
nothing is harmless to a troubled boy.
Each small innocent "something" is insidious
to a sensibility so fastidious
I could not as a child pick up a ball
less than a thousand times, if at all.
Please Please PLEASE consider my plight:
I can do NOTHING just once, just, twice, or just right.
All is uncertain. Uncertainty is bliss.
I would never have CHOSEN a life like this.
But no one cared that I counted to ten
again and again and again and again –
I cannot remotely remember when
as a child or a man I did not count to ten.

OCD, Explained

My brain: a pound of jam
in a bowl of bone
irrigated with blood, alive.
Full of mischief and secrets
bubbling with ways to make the world
more beautiful—a poet's brain!
Obsessive-compulsive to a fault.
A thought in my hand as fragile as
a baby, minutes old, wailing
slimy, survival in the balance—
every thought I have is like that
soft-skulled, impossibly tender
and every idea, a cupped handful
of water I tremble to contain.

The Weight of Spring

Spring is a dangerous time
for the suicidal, I am told.
I tried it once myself and yes
It was April. My demons had lain dormant
all winter long: fragrant aromas
arose from the earth, rousing
them from their slumber . . .
it is a mistake to believe that beauty
holds no menace, to sniff a rose
and feel that all is well
with the world. I slashed my throat
on the evening of the loveliest day
walking in the benevolent warmth
of the sun. A "psychotic break"
they called it; I was overwhelmed
with the weight of everything magnificent
in the world; strange how happy I was
all that afternoon. It was evil
that did it. Sophisticated people do not believe in evil so
I will not try to convince you.
Let's just say that I lived,
that I spat in Satan's face
in my anguish to survive.

Notwithstanding

My poor long-suffering therapist
has listened to a mountain of woe
for many years. How can he stand it
week after week, with my litany
of suicide attempts, OCD,
depression, exhilaration and
various fears real or imagined—
I have loaded all my demons on
to his plate. He knows them better than
I do. My therapist's name is Scott:
no less than an angel in my book.
It would come as no surprise at all
to him, that amidst my pain and strife
it truly is a wonderful life.

Would-Be

I stood at the threshold of death
and peered inside. The door was slammed
in my face, curiosity
unfulfilled. I smelled a sweetness
in the air. The fragrance of death
filled my lungs. I was not wanted
on this particular day. I
had no fear whatsoever. I
focused my attention on life;
I had seen just enough to know
Death is merely another door
To walk through when I am allowed.
It is one I can slip through when
Invited, and close behind me.

Man Up

There's something I don't trust
about reality (I can't quite
put my finger on it). How
it's sometimes too good
to be true, sometimes
too awful to bear.
I have turned my back
on reality so many times.
Even tried the coward's
way out—that didn't work.
I guess I must "man up"
put my nose to the grindstone
and tough it out.
Face the immutable fact
that reality is here to stay.
It's not going anywhere
anytime soon.

Untitled 7

My problems are no concern of yours.
So why the hell do you read my poems?
Have you too attempted suicide?
Have you too had a nervous breakdown?
Do you feel better by comparison?
Can't you see that I have no answers.
I live my life one day at a time.
Yes, I am a stalwart friend of Bill's.
My sobriety has saved my life.
I am drawn to confessional poets.
They can make art out of misery.
I think that's really a neat trick.
Yes sir, my troubles are all my own.
So why don't you just leave me alone.

Enough Said

Of course it was a cry for help:
Do you suppose I did not know
how to slit my own throat
and get the job done right?
I'm sorry for the spectacle I caused
and for the mess on the kitchen floor.
Sometimes you just do what you must do.
Sometimes you just can't take it anymore.
So there you have it, my apology.
Sincere. Succinct. Firmly from the heart.
Sorry to give my loved ones such a shock.
No regrets at all I did not succeed.
Thank you, thank you from my very soul.
Life is now quite pleasant, on the whole.

Note to Therapist 1

There's a point to which I cannot go
despite how well-intentioned you are.
A certain amount of my psychoses
must stay with me to the bitter end.
It clings to me like a childhood friend
whom it would be cruel to leave behind.
You have helped me grope my rocky way
into the future. You've given me a life.
I cannot make the ultimate betrayal
which being well requires me to make.
I will always be at a kind of stand-off:
I will never let go of your hand.
My other hand grabs with rash loyalty
a boy who'd destroy me, given the chance.

Credo

I bloodied my knuckles
to get where I am
Against a stone wall
to get where I am

I wrung out my heart
to get where I am
like so much laundry
to get where I am

I am nothing but scars
and scabrous peeling
I am always wounded
and always healing.

April, 2010

There was a touch of evil
to my suicide attempt.
Demons skulked in the walls, My
life became a proxy fight
of evil vs good. The hand
maneuvering the knife was
not my own. My closest friend
was called upon to wrestle
Satan. My surgeon asked Gary
if I was a religious
person: a physician shocked
that he saved me, pulled me back
from the abyss. That was ten
years ago. Christ, it was close.

Untitled 14

Slumming at Starbucks
sipping my overpriced
but Fair Traded coffee
I work at my craft.
I realize my job
is to present the world
in the best possible
light. I believe in God.
This does not endear
me to my kind: we are
supposed to imagine
the world merely exists
on a devil's whim—light
and grace are accidents.
The world is a bad place
despite my feeble attempts
to convince you otherwise.
I am an oddball.
I am a contrarian.
I am a failure.

Bacon

Pigs flew in my dreams last night.
Something amazing must have happened
in the world. A cure for cancer?
The Second Coming of Christ?
It was a startling image:
an airborne brigade of hogs
flew two abreast with military
precision (yes, they'd sprouted wings)
over Secaucus, New Jersey
where once there was a famous pig farm—
Maybe they flew for me. Perhaps
I'd been cured of OCD
after sixty years. But I looked down
and Hell had not yet frozen over.

At the Zoo

At the zoo I couldn't help but think
how I too was once on display
at the orphanage. All of us
were eligible for adoption:
prospective parents would visit
every Sunday. I never made the cut.
I had a reputation for being wild.
The nuns—God damn them—would smile
and laugh as potential parents said
incessantly isn't he cute isn't he cute
I got sick of hearing it so
I sunk further into OCD.
I'm grown up now, not for sale—
still wild, but happy to be free.

Dead of Night

My guardian angel
takes another cigarette break—
he deserves it. I feel
a new, strange kind of peace
come over me. Fifty
years, I have barely been
in his sight. The poor long-
suffering bastard knows
I can handle it.
Something is different.
Oops—he's coming back.
I shouldn't be awake.
Don't want him to know
that my demons are dead.
By the way, his name's Fred.

Healing

I don't use public toilets.
What self-respecting germaphobe
would think of doing such a thing!
I don't share bathrooms either.
If I don't have my own bathroom
at the place I'm goin', I ain't goin'.
My therapist is very proud of me:
He knows I've made a certain peace with germs.
He insisted from the very start
we must live with a certain amount
of germs. I thought at the time:
easy for him to say. Today
I stared a germ right in its face—
told it to go to hell. Where it came from.
The little monster fled down the toilet.
I smiled in antiseptic triumph.

Fear

"Nothing is to be feared,
only understood," said Marie Curie.
Wise woman. I have been
working on overcoming fear
all of my life and only now
do I know: fear cannot be fought.
It will always win. It will mock
your feeble attempts to reason
with it. It is a parasite
that feeds on you like a tapeworm.

Fear begins to loosen its grip
when your need to understand it
is even greater than your courage.
Fear begins to lose the minute
you get fiercely curious
about it: when you shed light
on the bastard let the world
see it naked.

Man With OCD on Ocean Liner

I want to throw myself overboard.
This is what is known in the trade
as an intrusive thought. No kidding.
I imagine myself swallowed up
by the fierce, rolling sea. I used to be
afraid of thoughts like this. I was also
obsessed with throwing myself in front
of a speeding New York subway train.
My therapist said: Don't judge the thoughts
or judge yourself for having them ...
Tonight there is a full moon over
the Aegean. I work very hard to do
what my therapist says. I stay on board.

My Germs

They are the confetti, the fairy dust
of Satan. I wash my hands
And feel them swirling down the drain to hell.
I look in the mirror at a man
distraught with cleanliness. No germs like that
can kill me, my therapist emphasized.
And I said "Killing me is not the point.
They want to make me miserable."
Then you must kill them with kindness, he said.
Wash your face in the toilet. Lick the rim.
Show them how you cannot live without them.
Make them feel important, truly wanted . . .
"That's gross. That's disgusting," I protested.
Then I suddenly saw his point, odd as
it was. I have washed my hands one million
times, not out of any real desire
to be clean, but out of fear.
I am emboldened, liberated, redeemed
this morning. I have loved my germs too well.
My hands are now empty and so sad.

My Psychotherapist

I place my psychoses in his lap
and with a thoughtless quick-of-his-hand
they become loose change in his pocket.
He is trained to absorb the most egregious
defects of the mind, immune
to the crushing existential burdens
men take on themselves. My sorrows
buy him his morning cup of coffee.
He trades my joys for a newspaper.
He is very good at what he does,
soaking up troubles. He sends me away
each week with a few less delusions.
He puts a little something in my pocket—
the gentle promise I will be well. Someday.

Note to Therapist 2

Something is missing,
either a piece
of my mind or of
my soul
(They're two very
different things)
Somehow I just
don't feel whole.
If I had to guess, I'd say
it's part of my mind that's gone—
just the sort of thing a poet
can capitalize on.

Obsessive Compulsive

At the age of twenty-five I stood
like a helpless, tragic fool in front of
the Port Authority Bus Terminal, trying
to get in—trying desperately to simply
get in and go home. I was lost
in a plague of failed maneuvers.
Nothing worked because I was trapped
in a cruel immediate past, paralyzed
by the fear of going forward
and the greater pain of standing still.

I felt commuters staring as they passed by
in a blur of color and speed, free as birds.
I felt the vagrant's pity when his eyes
gray and milky from lack of sleep, locked
onto mine: He knew I was cast in stone
and could not move, innocent and stricken
like a child of Pompeii encased
in the bile and flaming guts of Vesuvius.
I was merely a child chosen at random
for this odd and peculiar life, saved
at the end of the day only by darkness,
and the senseless, overriding need to face
the joyless music across the Hudson River.
I caught my bus, exhausted and dazed.

How could I ever have a child of my own?
Where would I find the blunt vigilance
a child requires? Imagine if I froze
at just the moment he chose to wander off
into the path of an oncoming bus.

How could I stand over his broken body
racked with failure and grief, begging the boy
to forgive his selfish, pathetic monster
of a father, this poor excuse for a man.

Note to Therapist 3

You are the wall I bang my head against.
You are the compulsion I give in to
without fear. You are the handful of germs
I blithely wash away. You are the man
I turn to when outlandish thoughts
of self-destruction tease me anew.
I could not get through this without you.
You are the buoy I swim toward
when I've gotten in too deep:
I embrace you tightly and I keep
my head above the water.
I understand how vulnerable I am
when in your presence. I renew my faith
in God and most importantly, myself.

Ode to Abilify

Millions rely on you each day
for peace of mind. Sweet, kind
Abilify! You get me through
the day with grace and finesse.
You're the secret of my success.
Who knows what mayhem might ensue
if I did not depend on you--
tiny little white pill daily
you keep me on the safer side
of sanity. Depression thwarted
and on the darkest of days
I have my own private sun.
Feel so good! Soar like an eagle!
How can you possibly be legal?

Reflection

I'd had it with suicidal poets.
I gave my Anne Sexton bio away.
Same with my Sylvia Plath.
I held their suicides against them.
Especially Sylvia. Pity those kids.

Until the night I tried it myself.
It was nothing I'd ever thought of.
That's what made it so scary.
I escaped within an inch of my life.
I was left with three visible scars.

Today I went to the Strand bookstore.
Bought both books I'd given away.
I have given up judging people.
Especially suicidal poets.

This is OCD

A man reads a book across the café
while lunching on a sandwich. I
am fascinated and horrified
at the same time: how could he let
himself do that? What if mayonnaise
or something should get on his book—
it would be ruined for sure. I want
to grab the book from his hand. I
want to show it proper respect.
When I read a book of my own
my hands are sacrosanct, as clean
as a saint's. A stain on a book?
A sacrilege! Doesn't he know that?
Do I have the guts to tell him?

OCD 2

This is zero hour. The time
to stop wrestling with the bear
has come. I gather my courage
and walk away, knowing I
am not a quitter. The bear,
you see, never existed, yet
he battled me to a draw
for years. One childhood monster
chased me into my adult years
when he should have gone to hell
where he belonged. Yes, I am through
with the fight. I blame God
for the whole thing. He let me suffer
and dared me to find meaning in it.

Untitled 1

Dr. Healey, God bless him, likened my plight
to that of Sisyphus, King of Corinth
whose hubris banished him to Hades
to roll a giant boulder up a hill
forever, to see it fall again and again…
  (It was a stark analogy
  to my relentless OCD)
Wise psychiatrist that he was, he knew
that Abilify, taken every day
and my own pugnacious persistence
would release me, in time, from my curse.
He taught me that life, while not splendid
was "good enough", that my intrusive thoughts
crazed and wicked, would go away--
Dr. Healey, to my horror, fell
off a ladder and retired
leaving me with a useless rock
that turned into a paperweight.
I never saw him again. He
had become my very best friend:
if not for him I would surely still
be rolling my boulder up the hill.

Untitled 13

7 years after my suicide attempt
everything seems under control.
I feel suspiciously whole.
My tears are no longer of regret.
There is nothing now I ache to forget.
I am willing to remember it all.
Willing to risk an emotional fall.
I feel courage seeping from every pore.
Truly, nothing can hurt me anymore.
I've borne this burden for 53 years.
A burden of manufactured fears.
I grew weary of protecting a child.
We two could never be reconciled.
I had to kill him: a knife to the heart.
Only then could my adulthood start.

A Dubious but Welcome Anniversary

April is safely behind me
now, ten long years of healing
body and mind, countless pills,
a lifetime of conversations
with a long-suffering shrink.
Haven't had sex for a decade.
The kitchen was so messy that night
my virus-undetectable blood
shooting like a wild garden hose
from my neck: ICU and three
operations to save my trachea.
The surgeon asked if I believed in
God. He couldn't believe his own hands
had saved me. So I whistled
so long ago, past the graveyard. I
tried to tell anyone who'd listen
that HIV and OCD could
not co-exist for very long. I
was a ticking time bomb. It was just
a matter of months before the knife
sliced open my throat. O, it all has
a happy ending, my viral load
still undetectable, OCD
under control. It's delightful to be
one less poet lost to suicide
during national poetry month.

End of an Era

This is the last "confessional" poem
I will ever write. I've bored the world
to tears with my musings on suicide,
mental illness, a lost childhood. God.
Starting now, I am looking outward.
Starting now, it is no longer
all about me. It's about you.
Now when it comes to God I have to
admit I'm obsessed beyond reason:
I cling to him like a drowning man
grasps a heroic lifeguard. And lives.
I don't care if you have faith or not.
I'm waiting. What do YOU make of this
wretched, astonishing life we share?

Breakthrough

I cried the day my germs disappeared.
I did not need them anymore.
My tears were sincere, and genuine.
It was time to be a grown-up now.
Time to put the things of youth aside.
They'd clouded my life for fifty years.
I'd stepped around them like land mines.
Toilets. Sinks. Trash cans. My own mouth.
Everything was contaminated
if I made one false move. Everything
bore an element of danger. Once
I understood they could not kill me,
they were as good as dead. Disinfected,
they went to suck the joy from someone else.

OCD (not)

I have cut the cord.
My OCD goes floating away
as if into outer space—
a complete disconnection.
I am now over here.
My OCD is over   there.
I am a living marvel of
modern medicine:
my serotonin level is
soaring. Lots of prayers
were said on my behalf, so God
deserves some credit although
my psychiatrist gets the lion's share.
He treated me from the beginning
as if I were a normal person,
as normal as himself, and after a while
I realized he was right.
I am normal as rain, normal
as tears. And I've shed quite a few
along the journey.

No Clouds Today

I'm surprisingly at peace today.
There seems to be a perfect storm:
I feel my meds doing their job
and keeping my anxiety low.
I want them to award the Nobel Prize
to the men and women who invented
Abilify. In truth, I feel no stress
at all, about anything, a miracle.
What on earth is happening to me?
Truvada gave me a new lease on life.
Poetry flows like a river to the sea.
If this is the day the Lord has made
I'm grabbing it by the balls, sober
and content—holding on for dear life.

OCD, Tamed

We've come a long, long way
together, myself and OCD. I
was a child when the journey began,
when OCD stopped to offer me a ride.
The very first lie it told me,
that I was born to suffer, hit home.
I started banging my head against walls.
I was terrified of my mom dying
if I didn't hold my breath and count
to a hundred. And oh, how I counted
like a mad man, back against the wall!
I always lived with the certainty
that something terrible would happen
if I didn't bow to its sick pleasures.
As a grown-up, I signed a shaky truce
with OCD. I stopped demonizing
my own thoughts. I learned how to breathe.
My mother just turned 92 years old.

Factoid From the OCD Conference

Thirty percent
of American males
wipe themselves
standing up.

Seventy percent—
a clear majority—
sit down on the job.

Journal Notes: Anxiety

It's a puzzling neurosis.
It can kill in large doses.
Lesser amounts can bring you to your knees,
ruin the very day you want to seize.

It's a nasty affliction.
It causes much friction
between your will and your need to obsess—
all in all, it is one elegant mess.

Untitled 4

I once was fatalistic.
Almost became a statistic.
Then I got realistic:
You idiot, you're just artistic

Untitled 8

Took my clonazepam.
I might smile at you today.
I might not mean it.

Untitled 11

I am financially, morally
and emotionally stable.
I'd be a big bore
at your table.

If you want your party
to be a winner
invite a schizophrenic
to dinner.

Fires

When you have OCD
you are always putting out fires
that flare up round-the-clock:
compulsive little fires
that drive you crazy
and the sad irony
is that you yourself
are the arsonist.

OCD 1

OCD is like
arm wrestling with your brain—
neither side winning.

Untitled 9

I started out
to be a sundial
but I was so wound up
I became a clock.

The Last OCD poem

A knife in the sink
makes me stop and think:
what if I tried it again?
I wouldn't survive
or come out alive—
I think I'll just wield my pen.

ACKNOWLEDGMENTS

These poems originally appeared in the following publications, sometimes in different versions or with different titles.

alleykat's fishwrap: "Mental illness"

Backstreet Review: "Cousin Gloria," "Dead of Night," "My Psychotherapist," "One Week in My Life," "Reflection," "This Is Not a Pleasant Poem," "Would-Be"

Cheap Seats Ticket to Ride: "Note to Therapist 2," "Untitled 11," "Untitled 12," "Untitled 14"

Crazy Child Scribbler: "This Is Not a Pleasant Poem"

HIV Here and Now: "A Dubious but Welcome Anniversary"

International OCD Foundation Newsletter: "OCD 1"

ABOUT THE AUTHOR

Dennis Rhodes is the author of *The Letter I* (Chelsea Station Editions, 2014), *Entering Dennis* (Xlibris, 2005) and *Spiritus Pizza & Other Poems* (Vital Links, 2000). His poems and essays have appeared in *BLOOM, Chelsea Station, Lambda Literary Review, The Cape Cod Times, New York Newsday,* and other journals. Rhodes served as literary editor of *Body Positive* magazine and later as poetry editor of *Provincetown Magazine.* He co-founded the Provincetown Poetry Festival in 1999. For a number of years, he hosted a weekly radio show on WOMR in Provincetown, featuring interviews with local poets. He currently lives in Florida.

ABOUT INDOLENT BOOKS

Indolent Books is a nonprofit poetry press based in Brooklyn. Indolent publishes innovative, provocative, and risky work by poets and writers who are queer, trans, nonbinary (or gender nonconforming), intersex, women (of all races and ethnicities), people of color (of all genders), people living with HIV, people with histories of addiction, abuse, and other traumatic experiences, and other poets and writers who are underrepresented or marginalized, or whose work has particular relevance to issues of racial, social, economic, and environmental justice. We also focus on poets over 50 without a first book. Indolent is committed to an inclusive workplace. Indolent Books is an imprint of Indolent Arts, a 501(c)(3) charity.